My Little Book of
Big Trucks

by Honor Head

QED Publishing

Designed, edited and picutre researched: Starry Dog Books Ltd

Copyright © QED Publishing 2015

First published in the UK in 2015 by
QED Publishing
A Quarto Group company
The Old Brewery,
6 Blundell Street,
London,
N7 9BH

www.qed-publishing.co.uk

A catalogue record for this book is available from the British Library.

978 1 78493 013 4

Printed in China

Words in **bold** are
explained in the
glossary on page 60.

Contents

What are trucks?

Trucks are big vehicles used to move heavy **goods** and **cargo** from one place to another.

⌃ **The driver sits in a** cab **high up so he can see all around.**

≫ A truck's extra wheels help it carry heavy loads.

The cargo is carried on a **trailer** behind the cab. Most trucks travel thousands of kilometres, but some trucks, such as forklift trucks, stay at their workplace and don't go far.

⌃ **Big trucks need very powerful engines.**

Articulated lorry

An **articulated** lorry, or big rig, has two parts. The cab and the **semi-trailer** are joined together.

⌃ **Some articulated lorries have curtain sides, which make them easier to load.**

>> **Curtains are kept in place by strong straps and buckles.**

A semi-trailer only has back wheels. Its front end is supported by the cab. The truck can bend where the two join, so the cab turns a corner before the semi-trailer.

Rigid truck

These trucks are connected behind the cab. The cab and the back are all one piece.

⌄ **This rigid truck is carrying horses.**

⌃ **A strong metal frame, called a chassis, holds the truck together.**

The part of the truck used for cargo is called the body. Its weight is supported by the chassis.

≪ The cab has a cosy sleeping space for the driver.

Road train

A road train is a truck that pulls lots of trailers joined together.

« **This road train is carrying salt.**

A record-breaking
road train was
112 trailers long!

Road trains travel along
the highways of remote
places, such as the
Australian outback.

Flatbed lorry

A flatbed lorry has a trailer that looks just like its name – a long, flat bed. This trailer doesn't have any sides.

« Spare wheels can be lowered and used if the load is very heavy.

⌄ This flatbed lorry is moving a whole house!

OVERSIZE LOAD

Flatbed lorries are used to move goods that won't get damaged by rain or sun. The load has to be carefully strapped down to stop it falling off.

⌄ **Extra-wide wing mirrors help the driver see past the load.**

Petrol tanker

A vehicle that carries liquids is called a tanker. Tankers transport milk, oil or petrol.

⌄ The tanker body has round sides, like a can.

« Liquids are pumped in and out through special pipes.

Some tankers carry a cargo, such as petrol that could explode if there was an accident. The drivers are specially trained to put out fires.

⌃ **Tankers carrying dangerous liquids have a warning sign.**

Timber lorry

Flatbed lorries are used to carry logs. They travel from the forest to the factory, where the logs are made into goods.

⌃ The lorry's crane arm lifts the logs on and off the flatbed.

⌃ Special tyres allow the trucks to go off-road.

Timber lorries have tall steel **girders** along their sides. These stop the logs from rolling off when the lorries are driving.

^ These lorries often work in places that are hard to reach.

Car transporter

The biggest car transporters can carry up to 12 cars at a time!

⌄ **Most car transporters have two loading ramps, but some have three.**

« **The straps go through the gaps in the wheels.**

Car transporters move new cars from factories to showrooms. Chains and straps tie the cars to the trailers.

» **Driving a car onto the ramp takes a lot of skill.**

Tow truck

A tow truck or breakdown lorry, is used to rescue other trucks and cars when they break down on the road.

⌃ Strong steel legs stop the truck from tipping as it lifts its load.

A tow truck has lots of special equipment to help it remove cars from accidents, ditches, mud or water.

⌄ **Flashing lights warn other drivers of danger.**

⌄ **The lorry has steel cables, a** winch **and lifting ramps.**

Concrete mixer

A concrete mixer has a huge drum filled with sand, gravel and water.

⌃ Water is stored in a tank behind the cab.

>> The truck mixes the concrete as it drives to the site.

As the drum slowly turns, it mixes everything together to make concrete.

Concrete is used to make buildings, pavements and swimming pools.

⌃ A chute is used to pour the concrete.

Dumper truck

Dumper trucks are the biggest and heaviest trucks in the world.

⩔ **Dumper trucks are so big that the driver has to climb steps to reach the cab.**

Tipper trucks clear away rubbish or transport loads on building sites. They are also used to move coal.

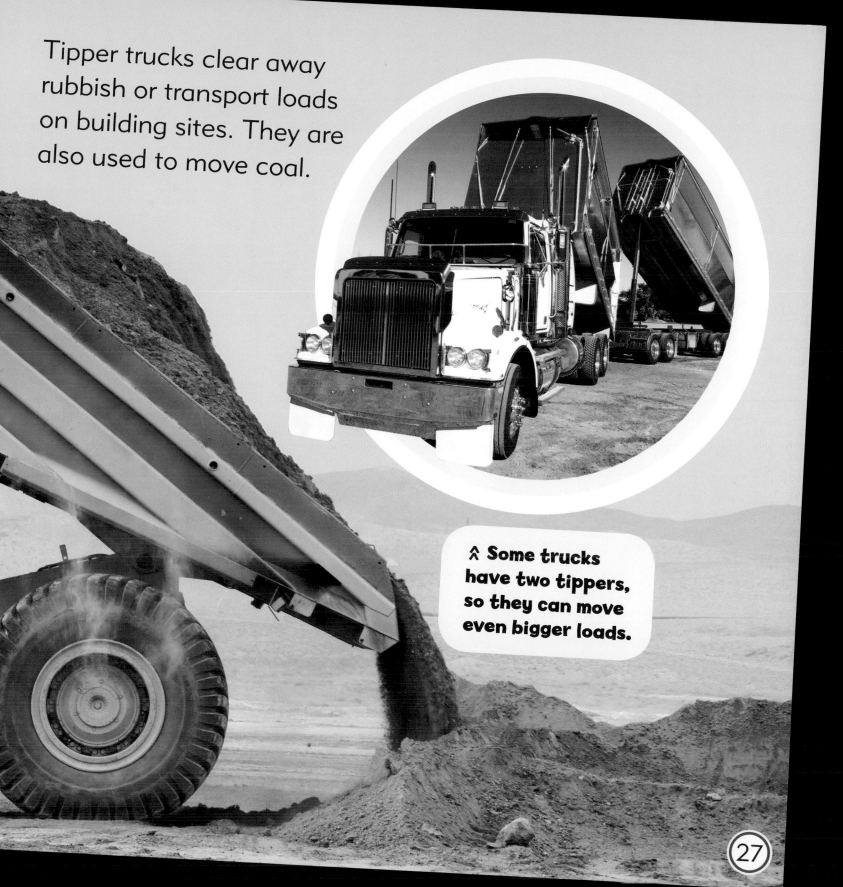

> ⌃ Some trucks have two tippers, so they can move even bigger loads.

These huge trucks work in **mines** and **quarries**, carrying rock. The rock often contains valuable metals, such as copper.

> ⌃ Giant dumper trucks are loaded by even bigger machines.

> « The very biggest dumper trucks cannot leave the mines because they are too big to go on normal roads.

Tipper truck

The body of a tipper truck tips up so the load slides off where it is needed.

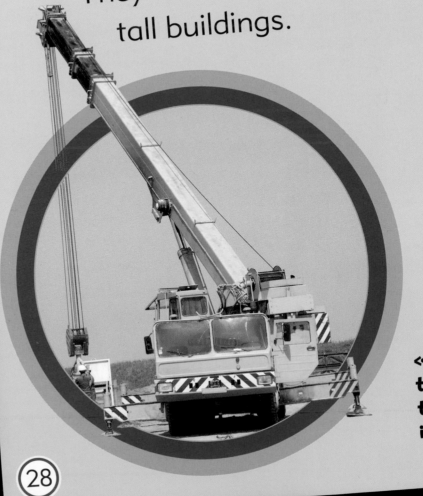

>> The back of the truck lifts up to tip the load out.

⌃ **Some trucks tip sideways.**

Crane truck

These trucks have a special arm that can lift huge weights. They are used to build tall buildings.

« Stabilisers **steady the crane** when **the arm is extended.**

Tipper trucks clear away rubbish or transport loads on building sites. They are also used to move coal.

> ⌃ Some trucks have two tippers, so they can move even bigger loads.

Crane truck

These trucks have a special arm that can lift huge weights. They are used to build tall buildings.

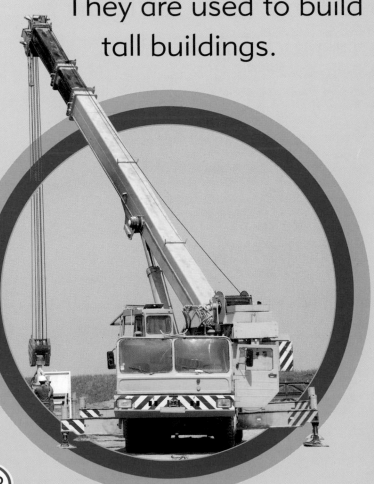

« Stabilisers **steady the crane when the arm is extended.**

⌄ When the truck is driving along, the arm is folded down.

With its arm extended, the tallest crane truck can reach 126 metres high and lift a load of up to 1.2 million kilograms.

⌃ Each wheel is nearly 2 metres tall.

Digger

Diggers are also called excavators. They can pull up trees, scoop up earth or knock down buildings.

ꙮ **Crawler tracks work better than wheels on rough ground.**

ꙮ **The engine is behind the cab.**

Diggers are used with dumper trucks to clear away earth and **rubble** in mines and quarries and on building sites.

ʌ The bucket has strong teeth for digging.

Bulldozer

Bulldozers sound big and strong – and they are! These mighty machines are also called earth movers.

« A ripper at the back breaks up the ground.

>> The blade is used for pushing earth, sand or heavy objects.

The blade at the front can clear forests or move huge mounds of earth to make the ground flat.

Compactor

This truck works on **landfill sites**. It is used to crush mounds of rubbish, so more can be piled on top.

« The metal spikes on the wheels tear the rubbish and press it flat.

Compactors have special wheels to do their job. The wheels are huge, heavy and spiked. As they drive over the rubbish, they break it up and squash it, so it takes up less space.

≪ **The cab has windows on all sides so the driver can see all around.**

≪ **The blade is used to spread waste mounds into flat layers.**

35

Drill rig truck

Some trucks carry a drilling **rig**, which is used to dig deep holes in the ground.

⌃ **When the truck is moving, the drill is carried flat.**

>> At the site, the drill is tipped upright for drilling.

Drilling rigs make water and oil wells and help build underground structures, such as tunnels.

⌃ Stabilisers keep the truck steady when the drill is being used.

Loader

These hard-working machines have a bucket in the front for scooping up earth or gravel.

>> **The driver uses a lever to move the bucket.**

Loaders are used to clear ground or dig holes. They load earth or gravel into trucks, which take it away.

<< **The bucket scoops up its load.**

>> **This load is being tipped into the trailer of a road train.**

Forklift

This fast little truck is used to pick up and move bulky loads short distances.

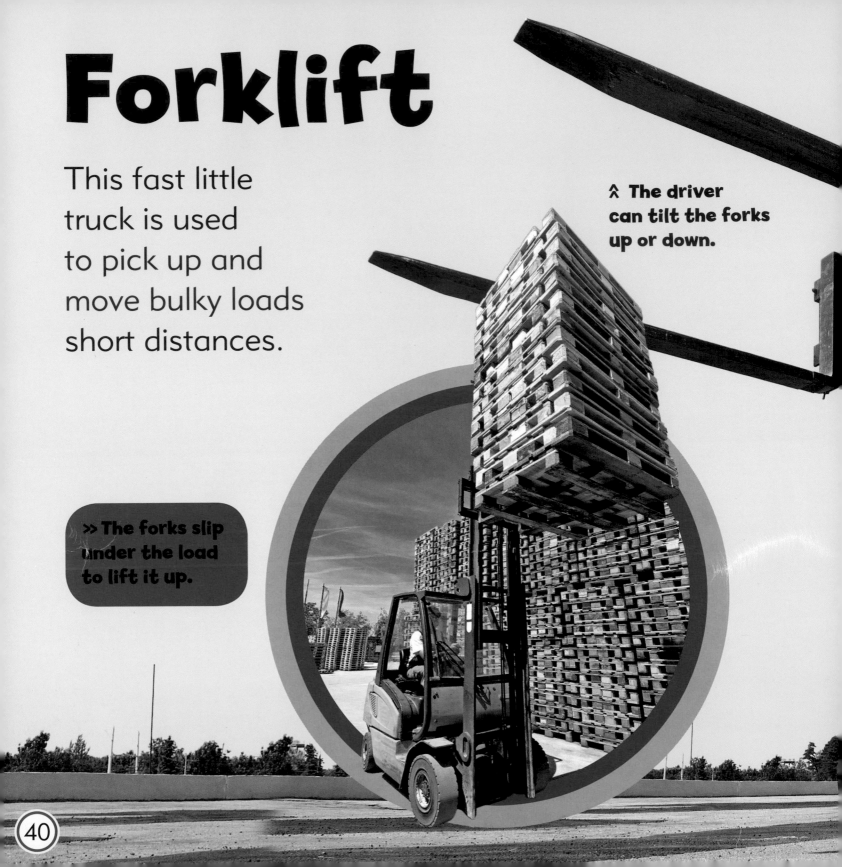

∧ **The driver can tilt the forks up or down.**

>> **The forks slip under the load to lift it up.**

‹‹ The engine is under the driver's seat.

Forklift trucks are used indoors in warehouses and factories. They are also used outdoors on building sites.

Robot truck

Giant, driverless robot trucks have been programmed to work in huge mines in Australia.

⌄ **The trucks use** sensors **to avoid crashing into each other.**

DT5310

⌃ **Each truck can carry up to 320 tonnes.**

>> The trucks are controlled by a computer in space.

The trucks work in mines, but are controlled from offices over 1500 kilometres away!

Tractor

Tractors are slow but powerful machines. They are used on farms to pull other machinery.

˅ **A hole in the back of the tractor provides power for the machine being towed.**

˅ **This tractor is towing a machine that makes hay bales.**

Tractors pull machines that plough fields, plant seeds, cut hay and make hay bales. Driving a tractor takes a lot of skill.

☆ Some tractors do not have a cab.

Combine harvester

⋁ Inside the drum, the grain is separated from the stalks.

A combine harvester is used on farms to gather crops, such as wheat or corn.

⋀ The spinning blades in the front cut the crop.

The combine cuts the crop, separates the grain from the stalks and pours the grain into another truck that drives alongside.

⌃ **The grain pours out of a long chute.**

Truck racing

Trucks not only do special jobs. They can also be fun to race. Truck races are watched all around the world.

⋁ Trucks can race at up to 160 kilometres per hour.

Trucks of all sizes are used for racing. Drivers need to be strong to control their trucks as they race around the track.

>> **The driver is protected by a helmet and by metal bars in the cab.**

Monster truck

Monster trucks have a normal-sized body but extra-big wheels.

˅ Car crushing is a favourite event at monster truck shows.

˄ Monster trucks jump from ramps into the air.

These trucks are specially built to thrill the crowds at truck shows. The tyres are often as tall as a normal-sized car!

> ⌃ **Monster trucks can even do wheelies!**

Pro-jet truck

This truck has **jet engines** like an aeroplane that allow it to reach very high speeds.

>> Pro-jet trucks usually race on their own to see how fast they can go.

⌃ The driver wears a special fire-proof suit.

The pro-jet truck shoots forward from the starting line. It can reach a top speed of 240 kilometres per hour.

Snow plough

These trucks save lives by clearing dangerous ice and snow from roads.

⌄ **Snow ploughs push the snow aside.**

⌃ **Sometimes snow chains are used to give extra grip on icy roads.**

Snow ploughs are used in countries that have a lot of deep snow each year. They help to clear the roads so cars and buses can run normally.

>> Some snow ploughs spread salt, called grit, on icy roads to melt the ice.

Amphibious truck

An amphibious truck is a truck that can be driven on land and in water.

⌄ Tourist buses can now drive off roads and into rivers.

⌃ These trucks can move faster on land than in water.

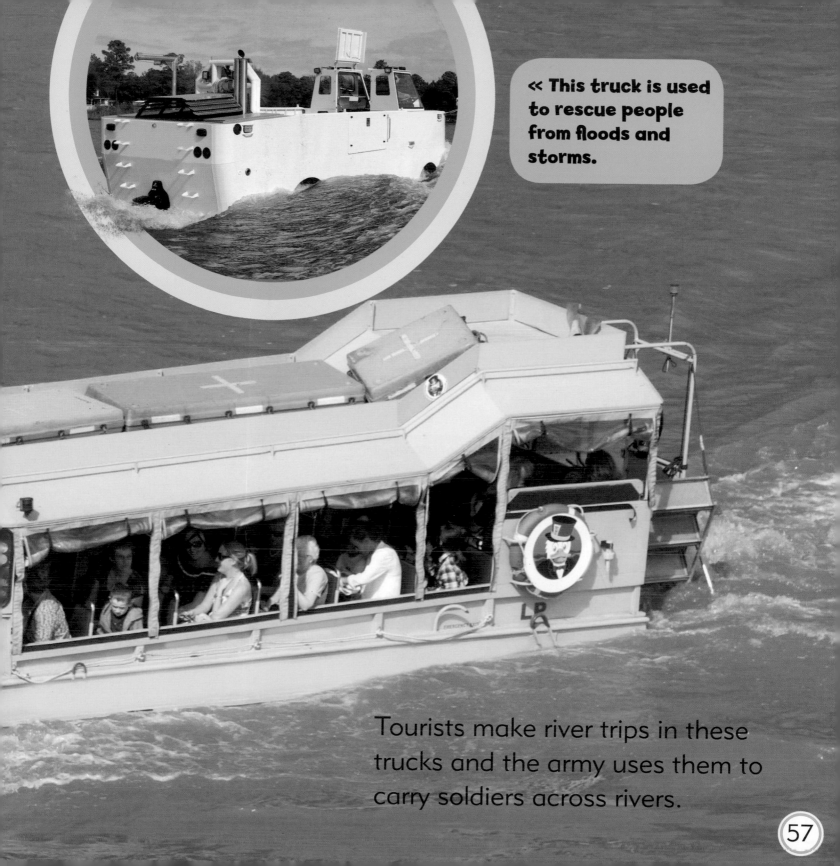

« This truck is used to rescue people from floods and storms.

Tourists make river trips in these trucks and the army uses them to carry soldiers across rivers.

Record-breaking trucks

From the biggest to the fastest, trucks have set some amazing world records.

⌃ **This 326 tonne Belaz dumper truck is one of the heaviest trucks in the world.**

The world's biggest truck is a dumper truck. It is 20 metres long and 8 metres high.

⌃ The world's biggest tyre is more than 4 metres tall.

⌃ The monster truck *Bad Habit* set the record for the longest ramp jump – 63.58 metres – in 2010.

Glossary

articulated Having two sections with a moving joint between them.

cab The front part of a truck, where the driver sits.

cargo Something that is carried from one place to another by truck, plane or boat.

chassis The steel frame that supports a truck's body.

chute A sloping pipe that things can slide down.

crane A tall machine used to move heavy objects.

engine Part of a truck that gives it the power to move.

girder A metal beam that supports a heavy object.

goods Items that will be sold in a shop.

jet engine A type of powerful engine used mainly by aircraft.

landfill site A place where rubbish is dumped and buried.

load A big, heavy thing that needs to be carried.

mine A place where coal or metals are dug up.

quarries Places where stone is blasted or cut from the rocks.

rig Equipment or machinery used for a particular job.

rubble Broken chunks of old stone, brick or concrete.

semi-trailer A vehicle with back wheels only. It has no engine and must be towed by another vehicle.

sensor A small machine that can tell if something is moving close by.

stabilisers Metal 'legs' that help keep a truck upright and stop it falling over.

trailer A vehicle with front and back wheels but no engine. It has to be towed by another vehicle.

winch A strong cable or rope used to lift or haul something heavy to a different place.

Index